Motivational Swear Word
Adult coloring book
for stress relief and relaxation
By Blue Moon Press House

THIS BOOK BELONGS TO:

....

....

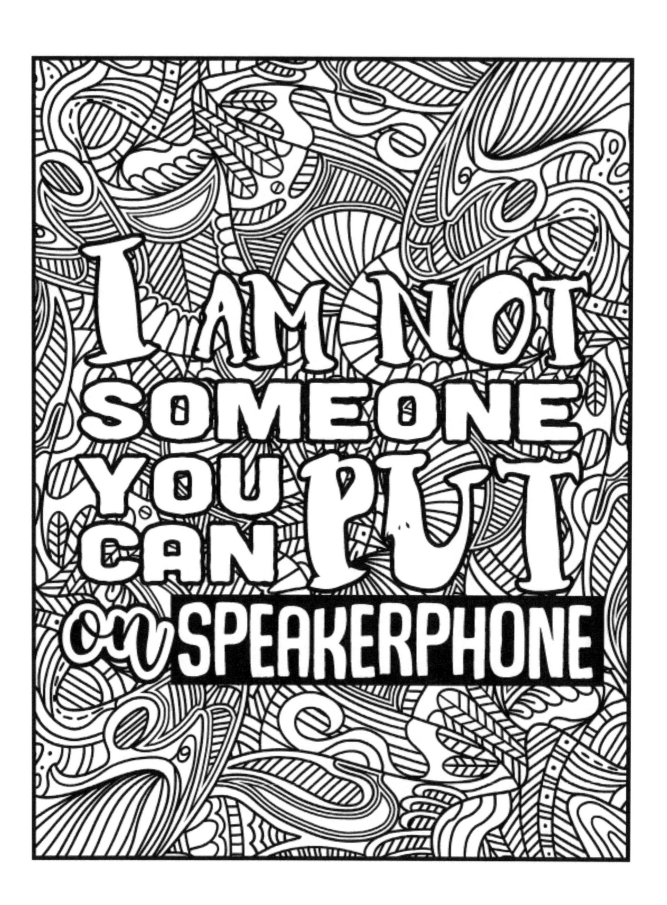

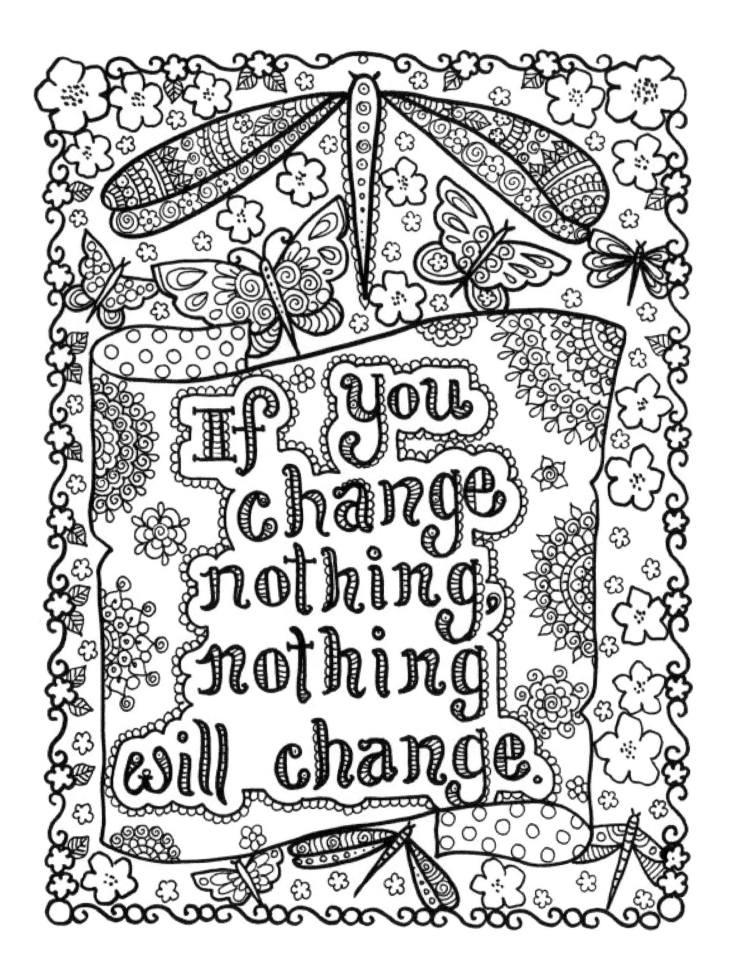

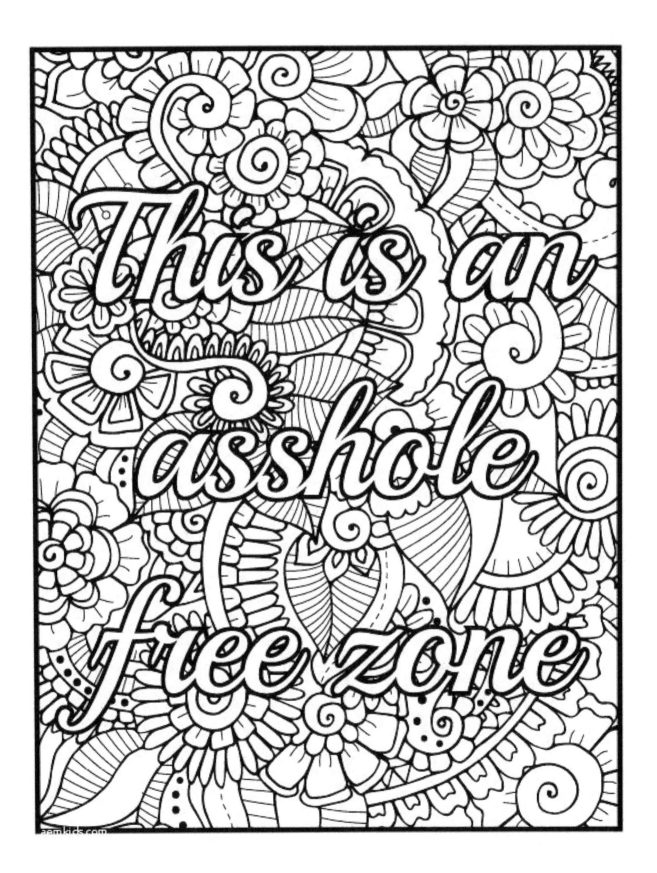

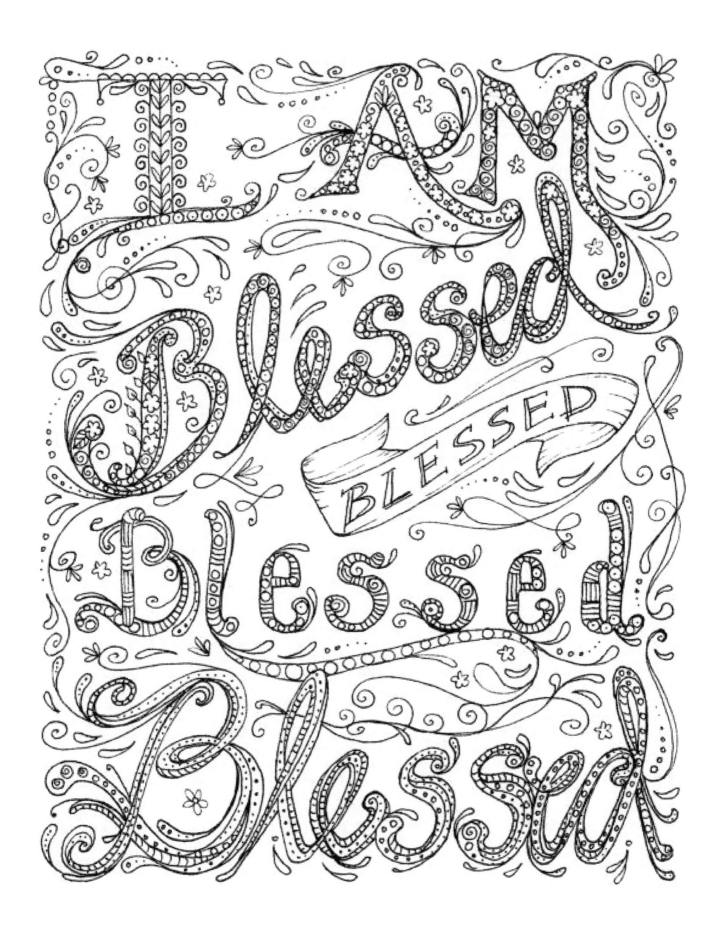

www.ingramcontent.com/pod-product-compliance
Lightning Source LLC
LaVergne TN
LVHW080050220125
801834LV00036B/1063